The Strange Story of Uri Geller

By
Jim Collins

A

Book

From
RAINTREE CHILDRENS BOOKS
Milwaukee • Toronto • Melbourne • London

Library of Congress Number: 77-24501

Art and Photo Credits

Cover photo and photos on pages 41 and 43, Globe Photos/James E. Enright.
Illustrations on pages 7, 10, 24, 28 and 31, Claude Martinot.
Photo on page 9, Photo Trends/Syndication International.
Photos on pages 11 and 32, Wide World Photos.
Photos on pages 14 and 37, Camera Press/Photo Trends.
Photos on pages 16 and 21, Shipi Shtrang/Kadima Productions, Inc.
Photos on pages 19, 46 and 47, "The News".
All photo research for this book was provided by Sherry Olan.
Every effort has been made to trace the ownership of all copyrighted material in this
book and to obtain permission for its use.

Library of Congress Cataloging in Publication Data

Collins, Jim.
  The strange story of Uri Geller.

  SUMMARY: Describes the psychic powers and abilities of Israeli-born Uri
Geller and presents the doubts of people who insist he is only a magician.
  1. Geller, Uri, 1946-   —Juvenile literature.   2.   Psychical
research—Biography—Juvenile literature.   3.   Magicians—Biography—
Juvenile literature.
  [1.   Geller, Uri, 1946-   2.   Psychical research—
Biography.   3.   Psychokinesis—Biography]   I.   Title.
  BF1283.G4C64   133.8'092'4   [92]   [B]   77-24501
  ISBN 0-8172-1037-7 lib. bdg.

Manufactured in the United States of America.
ISBN 0-8172-1037-7

Contents

Chapter 1
Uri Catches Britain Bending   5

Chapter 2
The Road to Fame Has Curves   12

Chapter 3
1,375 Broken and Bent Objects
Can't Be Wrong!   18

Chapter 4
The Man Called Uri Geller   23

Chapter 5
Tests, Tests, and More Tests   34

Chapter 6
"The Geller Effect"—Point-Counterpoint   39

Uri Catches Britain Bending

This is the story of a young man named Uri Geller. As far as we know, it is a *true* story. When you read of Uri's incredible powers, you may not think it is a true story at all. That will be up to you.

If you don't believe in Uri Geller you will not be alone. Some people think he is a "fake." At best, they feel he is a very good actor-magician. Many more believe Uri is truly gifted with magical powers. Let's see what you think after you read about the mystery called Uri Geller.

Uri Geller has an unusual talent. He bends metal just by looking at it. He stops clocks from ticking just by thinking about them.

Uri Geller has been doing these amazing things for years. He says he does them without using tricks of any kind. His mysterious talent has been tested by scientists. He has shown his powers to millions of people around the world. While many have tried, not one person has been able to prove he is not what he says he is.

One night Uri Geller came to the attention of the entire world. It was in November, 1973. He was appearing on an English radio program called the "Jimmy Young Show."

Uri explained that he was quite young when he discovered his strange powers. He could bend keys and nails just by touching them lightly! He could make broken clocks start and working clocks stop by using his mental powers. Uri was just as surprised as his classmates and parents were. Most of his friends believed that he used tricks. Uri kept saying he did not.

Uri told how he used to stare at his watch during class, hoping for the time when recess would come. Suddenly, the hands of the watch would move to 12:00—the time for recess. Uri would start to head for the door, and the teacher would cry, "Uri, get back to your seat. It's only 9:00!" Uri would show the teacher that his watch said 12:00. He couldn't explain how the hands had moved by themselves.

Jimmy Young asked Uri to demonstrate his powers. Young took a thick key from his pocket and asked Uri to bend the key with his mind. Everyone in the radio station anxiously awaited the outcome. People listening at home grew quiet with expectation. As always, Uri was a little nervous. He knew that most of the time, he could bend the metal. But he also knew that he sometimes failed. As Uri stared at the key Young had put on the table, everyone was asking the same question, "Will it work?"

Suddenly, the silence was broken. Uri made an odd request. He asked the people who were listening to place a metal object (spoon, fork, or

Somehow, Uri's watch said 12:00, time for recess.
But the school clock only pointed to 9:00 A.M.

key) near their radios. He also asked these people to try to bend the metal using the powers of their minds. He instructed them, "If there are any broken watches in your house, please concentrate on them and try to make them work."

Then Uri began to work. Lightly, he touched Jimmy Young's key. Uri stepped back, taking his hand from the key. Amazingly, the key began to bend and kept bending for many seconds. Jimmy Young couldn't hold back his surprise! He stood up and shouted, "It's bending right in front of me. I can't believe it!"

If it's hard for you to believe that keys can be bent by the power of the mind alone, you will find what followed even more amazing. Telephone calls started pouring into the radio station in record numbers.

Listener after listener reported that silverware, keys, and nails were starting to bend too. One lady reported that she was stirring soup when the spoon suddenly started bending. A policeman said that several knives and forks had curled up as he was watching them. A watchmaker said that his tweezers had bent. From all over England, Scotland, and Ireland came more such reports. Watches and clocks that hadn't run for years started up!

When the show was over, news reporters surrounded Uri. They asked him to use his mind to bend their keys, spoons, rings—anything! And Uri *did!* Of course, the reporters tried to get him to explain his powers, but he really couldn't. Although he had been bending metal for years, *he didn't know how or why* he could do it.

The next morning, newspapers all over England carried headlines about Uri. Some of the headlines were funny—*"URI PUTS BRITAIN IN A TWIST,"* and *"URI CATCHES BRITAIN BENDING."*

Dora Portman was listening to Uri while she was stirring soup. Suddenly, her spoon started to bend by itself.

Listeners all over Britain called the radio station
to report strange happenings.

Everyone wondered what would happen next. So did Uri! That night, he was supposed to demonstrate his powers on television. This show would be an even greater test. Millions of people would be watching. There would also be two scientists on the show to see if Uri Geller really might have special mental powers. One scientist was John Taylor, a mathematician and teacher. The other was Dr. Lyall Watson, a biologist. Uri's demonstration had worked amazingly well on radio. But only Jimmy Young and the radio crew had actually *seen* Uri bend metal there. What would happen on television?

Uri shows a bent key to John Taylor, a professor at Birbeck College, London.

Chapter 2

The Road To Fame Has Curves

The name of the television show was "David Dimbleby's Talk-In." Dimbleby had brought a supply of forks, spoons, keys, and some broken watches to the studio. He had also drawn a simple picture. He put the picture in an envelope so that Uri couldn't see it.

As always, Uri was nervous. He realized that all eyes would be on him. What would happen if he failed. Uri knew he couldn't control his powers. Sometimes they worked, and sometimes they didn't. He also knew that there were many who wanted him to fail on television. These people didn't believe in Uri's powers. As he sat thinking, the lights flooded on. The show was on the air. There was no turning back for Uri Geller!

First, Uri was asked to guess the picture that Dimbleby had drawn and sealed in the envelope.

The power to read someone else's mind is called *ESP*. ESP stands for *Extra Sensory Perception*. Most people believe that we have just *five* senses. We can see, hear, smell, taste, and touch. There are others who believe that we have a sixth sense. They believe some of us have more of it than others. It is this sixth sense that gives certain people the power to read minds. ESP is becoming a *serious* science. The sixth sense may also give the mind the power to move objects. Uri Geller is believed to have a strong sixth sense. He believes he can see things on an imaginary "screen" in his mind.

Uri tried very hard to concentrate on what was in Dimbleby's envelope. He closed his eyes and concentrated on the "screen" in his mind. Slowly, he claimed, a picture took shape in his mind. The picture was ". . . a sailboat," he said.

David Dimbleby opened the envelope. Inside *was* the picture *of a sailboat!* Everyone was amazed. How could Uri know about the sailboat?

But more was to come. David Dimbleby picked up a spoon and held it between his fingers. Lightly, Uri touched the spoon. He stared at it. Almost immediately, the spoon started bending. And then, as the spoon continued to bend,

Broken clocks and watches cover a Geneva stage, waiting
for Uri's powers to make them work again.

another unbelievable thing happened. A fork,
lying near the spoon, started to bend too. But
how? With millions watching his every move, Uri
hadn't even touched the fork!

The show wasn't over yet. Uri turned his
mind to the broken watches on the table. Again,
almost at once, Uri's powers worked. The broken
watches all started ticking again—right before
the eyes of the television audience!

14

Both scientists on the show could hardly believe what they were seeing. As the broken watches started, Dr. Lyall Watson's watch stopped working. What could have caused all of this? What unknown force was at work here?

People from all over the British Isles had been watching the show. Again, many called to say that spoons and forks in their homes had started bending. Again, others said that their broken watches had begun working. Were they telling the truth? Or were they caught up in the magic of the moment?

Still, some people felt that Uri was a fake. Even though they had seen him on television, these people were not convinced. After all, many magicians pretend that what they do is real. But almost all admit that they use tricks and illusions to make "magic." Why not? They are proud of their tricks. It takes a great deal of practice and talent to become a really good magician.

There is *nothing* mysterious about a magician's "magic." It's only fun. Many people believe that Uri Geller is the greatest magician of them all.

All through his life Uri has had to face the same problem. Few people believed that he has special powers. Few believed that he is gifted with some mysterious force that enables him to bend metal and read people's minds. Psychic or magician? Which one is the real Uri Geller?

Right after the television show, a British newspaper wrote: "Any worthwhile magician could perform similar feats. But it would be trick-

Uri Geller holds an iron spike he has bent.

ery. Uri *must be genuine.*" Since that time, Uri Geller-believers have begun to multiply all over the world. But Geller never doubted his own powers for a moment. About those who doubt him, he has said, "I have learned to ignore those who say what I do is false. *I* know what I do is real, and that is what counts."

Part of the mystery of Uri Geller is trying to decide which side you are on. *Is* Uri Geller real? *Does* he have fantastic mental powers? Or is Uri Geller a fake? Just another good magician? Uri tells an astounding story of how creatures from outer space gave him his magical power. In this book, it will be up to you to decide whether what you read is fact or fiction.

The TV show was over. Uri was now world-famous. But England was only one stop on his tour. What awaited this man of mystery was a series of adventures, one after another. For Uri Geller, that winter would be full of "miracles."

Chapter 3

1,375 Broken and Bent Objects Can't Be Wrong!

Uri's next stop was Paris, France. He made several appearances on radio and television. With each show, he gained more fame, more fans, and more believers. It was all very exciting. But the event that made his French tour unforgettable would happen, not in France, but back in England. An English newspaper, *The Sunday People,* wanted to test Uri's power in an unusual way. While Uri remained in Paris, could he bend objects in England?

Uri said he would try. The English paper asked its readers to bring out spoons, forks, and watches and place them on their tables. At exactly 12:30 P.M., Sunday, November 25, 1973, the English would concentrate with Uri in a long distance meeting of the minds. With Uri's help, they would try to bend metal with their minds.

Uri observes utensils he has bent and broken.

At the planned moment, Uri, in France, shouted, "Bend!" while the people in England concentrated. For days, no one knew if the test worked. Then the letters started pouring in. More than a thousand were sent to the newspaper. From all over England came reports of broken watches that suddenly began to work and

19

of bent metal objects. Finally, when all the letters were read, the newspaper reported:

Clocks and watches restarted	1,031
Forks and spoons bent or broken	293
Other objects bent or broken	51
	1,375

After Uri's amazing performance from France, the British *Sunday Times* wrote, "If people really can bend metal by mind power, it will mean a revolution in science and our whole way of thinking." People everywhere were asking the same questions: Is Uri real? If he is not using tricks, how does he do it? One other question came to mind: What would happen next?

The next month, in that winter of miracles, brought Uri to the United States. Working with Uri was a newsman named Roy Stockdill. Uri had used his mind to bend Stockdill's mirror and key. The now world-famous Uri Geller was going to perform still another amazing feat for Stockdill.

With Stockdill was a photographer named Michael Brennan. Uri decided to try a new experiment. He took one of Brennan's cameras and left the lens cover in place. That way, no picture

Keys bent in the audience as Uri co-hosted
the Mike Douglas Show.

could be taken. But Uri was sure he could still take a picture. He would use his mind.

Using himself as the subject, he decided to shoot three rolls of film. Later the film was developed. Everyone expected the film to come out blank. Uri didn't. He *knew* the pictures would come out. And he was *right!* There in the middle of the second roll, were two photos of Uri. The pictures weren't very good ones. *But how could they have been there at all?* The best answer may be a newspaper headline that appeared the next day: *"URI'S MIRACLE PICTURES."*

Uri's next stop was Norway. Again he was on television to show psychic powers. He succeeded. Norwegian spoons and forks were no better in resisting Uri than the English were.

One night Uri was talking to a reporter. He tried to explain his powers. Gazing out of his hotel room at all the neon lights in the shop windows, he spoke softly. "You know, sometimes these energies are so strong that lights can go out."

At that very moment the city went dark. The power was restored quickly. Did Uri Geller make the lights go out that night in Oslo, Norway? Is there any real way to know?

By this time, you should have many questions about Uri Geller's powers. Does he perform real magic? Is he a psychic? Do you wonder what the amazing Uri Geller is like, simply as a human being? Where does he come from? If he has fantastic powers, when did they start? Where did they come from? How does he *feel* about them?

Chapter 4

The Man
Called Uri Geller

He was born in Tel Aviv, Israel on December 20, 1946. In Hebrew, his name means "Circle of Light." His father was a soldier. When Uri was young, his parents divorced. His mother remarried, and Uri lived with her. He has stayed close to both his mother and father all his life. Today his parents are proud of their son and confess they are amazed at his secret powers. But even they can offer no explanation.

Uri tells of something strange that happened to him when he was three or four years old. Near his house was a huge garden where he liked to play. To him the garden was a magical place. Sometimes Uri visited the garden with his father. But he was just as happy to go alone, to spend time with only his active imagination.

The silvery light drew closer and closer to Uri, bathing him with its brilliance.

Young Uri found peace in that garden. He remembers the wind rustling through the leaves and the sound of the small birds singing. And Uri remembers something else.

One day he was alone in the garden. Suddenly he heard a loud, high-pitched noise. It rang in his ears and kept him from hearing anything else. All at once, everything became still. Even the wind stopped.

Uri looked up. A brilliant silver light covered him. The light seemed to be everywhere. The sun became invisible. The new light drew closer and closer until it knocked Uri over. He passed out.

When Uri awoke he ran to tell his mother what happened. She was angry with him for playing alone in the garden. But she told him to forget about the bright light. It was nothing—just a child's fantasy.

Now Uri wonders. *Was it just a childish dream?* Could it have been his first contact with a spaceship from another world? Was that moment in the garden the beginning of his powers?

Uri believes that something important did happen to him that day in the garden. His memory of what happened is too strong for it to have been a dream. But, to a child, the most extraordinary happening can seem normal. And the most normal happening can seem extraordinary. Can you remember your first snow? The sudden miracle of huge white flakes falling from the sky. Can you remember the moment when a snowflake first touched your tongue? Did you know that it was water? For a small child, snowflakes and spaceships are both miracles and seem real.

Uri's mother worked during the day. Sometimes at night, she played cards with friends. At these games, they played for money. When Uri's mother came home at night, Uri would be able to tell her exactly how much money she had lost or won. At first his mother was amazed. But because Uri did this time and time again, she began to suspect that he was different.

Except for these strange incidents, Uri was a normal child. He played with his friends. He laughed and cried and went to school as all children do.

Not long after Uri started school, his father bought him a small watch. In school, Uri would sit and look at his new watch. He would hope that the time would move quickly toward lunch hour or "free play." One day Uri looked sadly at his watch. It was still a long time until recess. A moment later, Uri looked again. His watch said it was time for recess. But the clock on the classroom wall said it wasn't. That was the first time Uri remembers making the watch hands move just by using his mental power. At first, Uri didn't understand it. He thought his watch was broken. His father brought the watch back and gave him a new one. The same thing happened with the new watch. Uri could change the time on his watch just by thinking about it.

He began showing his powers to his classmates. Of course, they all thought that he was playing some trick. Uri tried to explain that he wasn't tricking them. No one believed him. The children made fun of him. They didn't know what to think, so they laughed at him. Uri didn't like being laughed at, and he soon stopped showing people his powers. When something strange happened to him, he just kept it a secret. For the first time in his life, Uri realized *he was different from everyone else.*

Today, there are people who say that Uri just made up these stories about his childhood. It's almost impossible to prove one way or the other. Maybe Uri did just dream about the garden. Maybe both of his new watches were broken and couldn't tell the right time —*Maybe.* Or it just may be that Uri was chosen to be someone special. No one knows.

Uri's stepfather, Ladislee Gero, was from the island of Cyprus. When Uri was eleven, he and his family moved to Cyprus. It was very far away from Israel. It was also very different. Uri wasn't sure how he felt. He hated to leave his friends and his home. But he did like the excitement of living in a new country. His own father had returned to army duty. Uri liked his stepfather. So, all in all, the move was not too frightening.

It didn't take Uri long to become happy in his new home. He was given two dogs as pets. He says, "When I saw them, I knew I'd be happy. They jumped all over me and licked me. I knew I was at home."

Uri entered a new school in Cyprus. But he still kept his powers a secret. He was afraid to show them to other children. But he remembers one time when his powers worked especially well. His stepfather had bought him a bicycle as a present. Uri had to wait until he was 13 to get the new bike. Every day, Uri would go to the garage to peek at the bike. It had a padlock on it. Uri

As Uri concentrated on the padlock, it fell to the ground.

decided to try his powers on the lock. He concentrated as hard as he could. Suddenly, the lock fell off. Uri rode off on the bike. It was the first time he had put his powers to work for himself. Uri was happy with the results. His stepfather wasn't.

Another strange thing happened to Uri in Cyprus. There were many caves on the island. Uri used to love to visit them. One day he got lost in a cave. He had gone through many different passageways, but couldn't find his way out. He was scared and wished that his dog was with him. Amazingly, from out of nowhere, came his dog, Joker. The dog led Uri safely out of the cave. Now Uri wonders how Joker knew that he was in trouble. Was it ESP?

When Uri was older, he began showing his classmates his powers again. At first they too thought he was playing tricks. When Uri bent forks and spoons, and no one knew how he did it, however, their laughter turned to cries of amazement. Years later one of his teachers wrote:

Uri Geller was a pupil of mine for five years in Cyprus. Even while so young he astonished his friends at the college with his amazing feats, i.e., bent forks, etc. The stories he told them of the wonderful scientific things that could and would be done by him seem to be coming true. I, for one, do believe in him. He was outstanding in every way, with a brilliant mind. Certainly one does not meet a pupil like him often . . . .

Yours sincerely,

[Paragraph Omitted]   (Mrs.) Julie Agrotis

It was lucky for Uri that his teacher did believe in him. He tells of other cases of ESP when he was young that could have given him trouble in school. A boy named Joseph Charles sat a few rows behind him. Sometimes, Uri and Joseph wrote the same compositions. Uri knew that he didn't cheat. Joseph's words just seemed to come into his mind. Mrs. Agrotis began to believe him.

When Uri was 18 years old, he graduated from high school. All along, he had tried to be like most of his friends. He had played sports and had gone to the movies with friends. But he was still confused. He knew there was something very different about him. Finally he decided to join the Israeli army. He would be a soldier, just like his own father.

War broke out while Uri was in the army. He was wounded in the war. A bullet tore into his arm. (Even Uri's powers couldn't turn away bullets.) But something strange *did* happen to him while he was in the army.

Although Uri's rifle wasn't fully assembled, he said it fired when the others did.

His group was given the order to spread out and open fire on the enemy. Uri knew that his rifle was empty. Worse, it hadn't even been put together, because parts of it had been lost. Yet, for some reason, Uri was able to fire his rifle! Even now he can't explain how such a thing occurred. Again—*did it really happen?*

There is no way of telling. But there's more.

Uri once had a friend named Shipi. Shipi told Uri that he needed someone to perform for the students at his school. The school was willing to pay some money to the performer. Uri thought

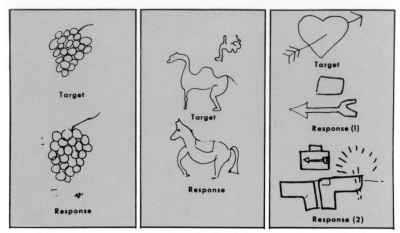

Uri responded to drawings he hadn't seen with matched
drawings of his own.

it seemed like a good idea. He could not only show people his secret powers, he would earn some money at the same time.

Uri has always wanted to be on stage. He likes people to notice him. During that first show, at the school, Uri didn't use his powers to bend metal or start watches. He presented only his ESP. The audience drew pictures and put them in sealed envelopes. Shipi held up each envelope, and Uri guessed at the pictures sealed inside. Most of the time Uri was right.

The audience was stunned. No one could understand how it was happening, not even Uri. But he was certainly happy. At last he found something that he really enjoyed doing. And he really enjoyed the applause too!

That day, Uri began his life as a psychic. From that moment on, he decided that he would never again hide his powers. The course of his life was now set.

Soon word spread about Uri's amazing feats. Everyone loved his shows. He would read people's minds and bend metal on stage. More and more schools wanted Uri to entertain. Then a news story about Uri appeared in a newspaper. Suddenly he had a lot of job offers. Soon he was appearing before large audiences in theaters and concert halls.

All Israel was buzzing with word of Uri. As usual, no one knew what to make of him. Uri kept saying he was *not* a magician. He simply had magical powers. But people demanded proof.

On August 17, 1971, Uri met Dr. Andrija Puharich, an American doctor and inventor. Dr. Puharich played an important role in the story of Uri Geller.

Puharich came to believe that Uri really did have strange powers. He set up scientific tests that would prove Uri's magical powers once and for all. First, Dr. Puharich performed some experiments himself. Then he took Uri to America to be tested at the Stanford Research Institute. Even an astronaut would get a chance to test Uri's powers. The results of those tests were astounding. But that's a story all by itself.

Chapter 5

Tests, Tests, and More Tests

The Stanford Research Institute (SRI) is located in Menlo Park, California. It is very well-known and highly respected. Many SRI scientists do work for the government.

At SRI, Uri met Captain Edgar Mitchell, an astronaut who had flown to the moon. Mitchell had studied ESP and was very interested in meeting Uri. Along with Dr. Puharich, Dr. Hal Puthoff and Russel Targ were the scientists who tested Uri.

Before the scientists could even begin, they got their first result. As they were about to connect an instrument that measures magnetic forces, they asked Uri to concentrate very hard.

Suddenly the needle on the instrument started moving, showing a magnetic force. *Uri had not yet touched the instrument.* The scientists thought that such a thing was impossible. However, they were learning that, when Uri Geller is involved, the "impossible" seems to happen.

They began testing Uri's mental powers with some ESP experiments.

The Dice Box Experiment. A single die was placed in a metal box. The box was then shaken. No one, not even the experimenter, could know what number the die would show. It was all left to chance. Uri had to call out the number before it was revealed. The experiment was repeated eight times. *Uri's grade—100%.* He had said the right number eight times.

The Hidden Object Experiment. Ten aluminum cans were placed in a row. An object was placed in one of the cans. Uri had to decide which can contained the hidden object. *His grade—100%.* He found the right can 12 times without error.

The Picture Drawing Experiment. Before the experiment, simple pictures were drawn on 3 x 5 index cards. The cards were then sealed in two envelopes and put in a safe. Still sealed, the envelopes were placed before Uri during the experiment, and he was asked to draw the pictures. Amazingly, the drawings exactly matched those in the envelopes . . . *another grade of 100%!* Uri did this seven times without error.

These were tests to measure Uri's ESP. You can test your own ESP ability. Have a friend secretly write down a number from one to ten. You must guess the number. Keep a record of the number of correct calls. How often did you guess correctly? If you were Uri Geller, you might guess correctly every time.

To make the experiment more difficult, have your friend do a simple drawing. Make sure it is hidden from you. You must concentrate. Try to "see" the picture with your mind. Then draw what you think you see. Compare the two drawings. Are they similar?

More tests were conducted at SRI. One instrument, for example, had a very delicate balance. It moved at the least pressure. Without touching the instrument, Uri made the needle move on the balance. It seemed as if someone or something was mysteriously touching the needle. Of course, no one was.

Not knowing that another man has chosen this shape, Uri
draws a triangle on a blackboard in front of a large audience.

Many of the experiments were recorded on film. There are movies of Uri bending spoons and forks. In them, Uri touches the metal lightly, and it begins to bend. At the end of his testing at SRI, the scientists said they had seen things "for which we have no scientific explanations." The results of the tests at SRI were published in a famous science magazine called *Nature*.

Scientists are very careful people. They like to conduct *many* experiments before they draw a conclusion. Is the special "power" Uri Geller claims to have, real? That is the question the scientists set out to answer. They decided that Uri *seemed* to be real. They would not definitely state it, beyond a shadow of a doubt. So the question goes on unanswered.

Chapter 6

"The Geller Effect"– Point-Counterpoint

Uri Geller's European tour of 1973–74 was, in almost every way, a "winter of miracles." In each country he met some new challenge. Everyone wanted to find the one different test that his powers could not beat. In Sweden, for example, his television shows were taped, to be played for the public after Uri left the country.

With Uri gone, the tapes were shown on Swedish television. The results were incredible. It was as though he were right there! People all over the country reported bent metal objects and clocks that started running again after Geller's taped shows. Just as the French, the English, and the Norwegians before them, the Swedish people were feeling what was now being called the "Geller Effect." This was the term used to describe the strange things that happened when Uri Geller was around.

The "Geller Effect" may describe what happened. But it doesn't explain *why* these strange things happened. In Denmark, Uri had his first "failure" on television. He was able to bend metal as usual. But he failed to start up five clocks.

Uri was confused and embarrassed. At least one of the clocks should have started up, he thought. Was he losing his powers—right there on Danish television? The mystery was soon cleared up. Uri was not losing anything. He had been tricked. The clocks could not possibly work. One, for example, had cement inside. Even the great Uri Geller couldn't fix a cemented clock!

By the end of his stay in Denmark, most Danes agreed with what one local newspaper had written about Uri. "It has been clearly indicated that Uri Geller has talents which must be described as the greatest revolution in the history of man."

Uri *does* fail sometimes. But what does "fail" mean? Uri says his failures prove that he is not a fake. If he were using tricks, Geller explains, he would succeed every time. Don't all magician's tricks work every time? Uri says that he can't control his powers. That's why he sometimes fails.

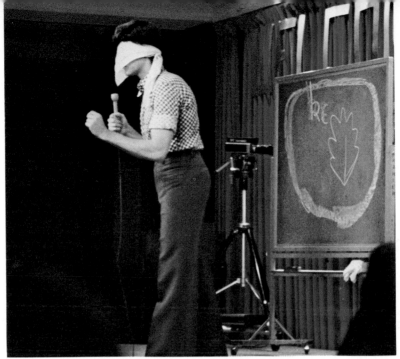

Uri performing in Rochester, Minnesota in 1976.

How can Uri be explained? Where does the "Geller Effect" come from? How can we be sure it's real? There are at least three answers that different people have given to these questions:

● *Uri Geller uses tricks the same way magicians do. There is nothing unusual about him.*

● *Uri has developed powers that we all have. ESP, the sixth sense, is something everyone has. Uri has just developed it better than the rest of us.*

● *Uri is helped by beings from another planet. These super-intelligent beings contact Uri and Dr. Puharich.* (This theory is the one Uri believes.)

One magician has given this answer:

"This Uri Geller—why, he is nothing but a magician, with a good gimmick. That's all. I don't see what all the fuss is about." Many magicians feel the same way about Uri. One of these, "The Amazing Randi," says that he can do almost everything that Uri does by using his own talent.

They point out that Uri often fails in front of magicians. Uri has had at least two famous failures. One was on Johnny Carson's *Tonight Show* shown on television. It was probably Uri's greatest appearance on American television. Nothing actually happened. Uri tried very hard, but his powers wouldn't work.

Uri says this proves that he *is* real. A "trick" should work *every* time.

Others have different feelings. Johnny Carson, an amateur magician himself, knows many of the tricks of magic. He had talked to Randi the Magician before the Geller show. "The Amazing Randi" told Carson what tricks to watch out for. Did Uri fail because he couldn't use his tricks on the Carson show?

Dr. Andrew Weil once believed in Uri. He had met Uri and watched him bend metal. That time it was a belt buckle. This was enough to convince Dr. Weil.

Then Weil met "The Amazing Randi." Randi says that there is nothing supernatural about his own tricks. They are simply illusions. Nothing more.

Randi did "one of Mr. Geller's favorite tricks." There were many metal cans placed on a table. Weil filled one can with nuts and bolts, while Randi was out of the room. Randi was able to pick the filled can, just by looking at them. No one else could do this. You may remember that this was one of the tests Uri took at SRI. Randi showed Weil the trick, but made him promise never to reveal it.

Uri bends a spoon before an audience in Rochester.

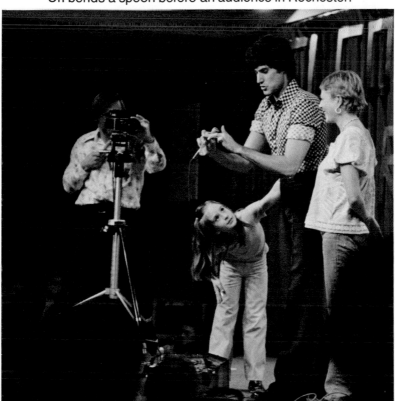

Then Randi picked a perfectly straight nail. He touched it lightly, just the way Uri does. The nail started to bend. Does "The Amazing Randi" have special powers? No, he uses a trick called "sleight-of-hand." At the very last moment, Randi substitutes a bent nail for the straight one. This is very hard. *But it is just a trick.*

Uri responds to this criticism by saying the magician *might* be able to do some of the things he does. But he makes two points: First, he says, they can't duplicate *everything.* What about the people in England who had spoons and forks bent just by watching the show? Uri says that he showed his powers to scientists who were on the lookout for tricks. He dares the magicians to go to SRI and be tested by scientists. Second, Uri says that he simply *does not use tricks.* He knows he doesn't and that is enough for him.

There is still another explanation for Uri's powers. There are many people who believe that we all have powers of the mind that we don't know about. Have you ever felt something was going to happen before it really did? Have you ever known what someone was going to say before the person actually said it?

These are all *possible* examples of ESP. There are cases of people receiving warnings before disasters happen. Some people claim to be able to read the future. Some of these mysterious powers have been investigated by scientists, but we still have no way of explaining them.

Maybe we all do have the power to bend metal with our minds. Or to read what is on other people's minds. Uri Geller may just have a stronger dose of this mind power. Most people can walk. But very few people can run a mile in less than four minutes. It takes a lot of talent and a lot of work. Maybe Uri is a "mind athlete." He started out with a lot of talent, and he worked on developing it to the fullest degree.

Imagine what the future would be like if we knew how to use such powers. Heavy objects could move just by using the powers of the mind. Maybe we would not need telephones if we could send messages just by thinking about them. Think of how your life would be different with such "mind power."

Uri thinks that this will not happen. After he met Dr. Puharich, he says, even stranger things began happening to him. According to Puharich, he and Uri have been singled out by a very advanced intelligence from outer space. These beings talk to Puharich.

Uri stares at key and concentrates very hard.

Uri tells of one weird event that happened to him not long ago. He was walking home to his hotel in New York City. Suddenly, it was as if he were lifted up and flown through the air. Next thing he knew, he came crashing through the screened window of Dr. Puharich's home almost one hundred miles away! What happened?

Puharich says that he accidently discovered the existence of beings from another planet. Puharich had hypnotized Uri. When Uri was deep in a trance, he told Puharich about what had happened to him as a child in the garden. He described the brilliant white light that had encircled him. Suddenly, Uri's voice changed. He was no longer Uri Geller. The voice seemed to come

Soon, the key is bent out of shape.

from somewhere else. The voice supposedly said:

> It was us who found Uri in the garden when he was three. He is our helper sent to help man. We programmed him in the garden for many years to come, but he was also programmed not to remember. On this day, his work begins. Andrija [Dr. Puharich's first name], you are to take care of him.

Since that time, Puharich says that he and Uri have had many other messages. The voices came from the *Nine,* super-intelligent beings who control the universe. One is supposedly the voice of a gigantic intelligent computer.

Most of the messages now are sent through Dr. Puharich's tape recorder. Puharich will put a blank tape in the recorder. Later, he will play the

47

tape. And a message will be on the tape! But no one else hears these messages!

Many of the messages are about Uri and Puharich. For example, a voice told Puharich to write a book and reveal the existence of the *Nine*. Another told him to make a movie about Uri. All of these are money-making projects for Puharich and Geller!

Both Uri and Puharich report seeing flying saucers and spaceships from outer space. Once Uri was on a plane. His camera was on his lap. Suddenly the camera rose up and took a picture—as if of its own will. When Uri developed the picture, he could see three flying saucers. However, there is no negative of the picture.

The rest of us have no real proof of any of this. How can we believe the existence of the mysterious *Nine?* How can we even believe in Uri Geller's mysterious powers? There are so many unsolved mysteries in our world. Uri Geller must be considered one of them. Perhaps we will *never* know the truth about him. Rest assured, there are people who will keep trying to find out.

For now, the question is to believe Uri or not. The choice is yours.